HOW TO MAKE
Garden Pools

THE DOUBLEDAY GARDEN HANDBOOKS

— Additional Titles in Preparation—

PUBLISHERS' FOREWORD

EACH YEAR increasing numbers of homeowners, both men and women, discover the satisfaction of gardening as an avocation that gives real returns in health, in the joy of creating beautiful home grounds, and in the greater monetary value that proper plantings give to all real estate.

If you want brief, direct, but reliable help with the handling of the seeds, bulbs, plants, and other garden materials that you buy from the seed store or nursery (or that your neighbors give you) this book is for you.

Like its companion Doubleday Garden Handbooks it is written for the owner of the small place who wishes to find quickly the specific help needed to make its particular phase of gardening successful and satisfying. The author is well qualified, not only to give reliable information from personal experience, but also to present it so as best to answer the questions of the busy amateur who prefers to do most of his (or her) own gardening. Even experienced gardeners, however, will find in this book many new suggestions and ideas.

Extensive lists and detailed descriptions of plants are not given here because they are to be found, well illustrated and described in any good dealer's catalogue. Your nearest seedsman or nurseryman will gladly suggest the best plant materials to use for your own climate and situation. Illustrations are entirely drawings, both to make possible the low price of these Handbooks and because they supplement and illustrate the author's suggestions much more clearly than could even the best of photographs.

This is a practical manual, designed to help you achieve maximum success and pleasure from the time and money you have to spend on gardening. Get the seed, bulb, and nursery catalogues of reliable dealers, consult those nearest you, and use this book to help you decide what types of plantings best suit your own place and purposes, how to plan and plant your garden, and how to care for your plants for best results.

As your garden interests multiply, add new Doubleday Garden Handbooks to your library to help you with the new phases which intrigue you. Complete your set gradually as you want help on various garden subjects, and keep them all together in your library or in your garden work-room for constant and repeated reference throughout the year.

A HEMLOCK
B RHODODENDRON OR LAUREL
C FERNS
D MOSS OR MOUNTAIN PINKS
E CUPRESSUS OBTUSA VAR. GRACILIS
F IRIS, DWARF
G SEDUM RUPESTRE
H PRIMULA

I AJUGA
J CREEPING JENNY
K WATER LILIES

FIG. 1. A GARDEN POOL WITH ITS PLANTINGS

This is the pool of which the construction is described in Chapter III. Rocks are arranged as stratified ledges (Fig. 18) and the plants grade up from small ones at the waterside to the background of trees and shrubs.

HOW TO MAKE
Garden Pools

BY
WILLIAM LONGYEAR

Illustrated by
THE AUTHOR

DOUBLEDAY, DORAN & COMPANY, INC.
Garden City 1935 New York

PRINTED AT THE *Country Life Press*, GARDEN CITY, N. Y., U. S. A.

CONTENTS

7

ILLUSTRATIONS

CHAPTER I

A Pool the Center of Garden Interest

THE pool does for the garden what the fireplace does for the living room. Both are pivotal points of family life and interest. In winter, we group about the open hearth with endless interest in the life and brilliancy of the moving flame. In the warm summer months, the cool ever-changing depth of the pool is equally fascinating.

The arrangement of furniture and accessories in the room frequently centers about the fireplace. It should be the same with the garden paths and borders in relation to the pool.

A few years ago I moved from a city apartment to a gray shingled colonial house on an average-size suburban plot. I found myself the enthusiastic and bewildered owner of a partially finished house surrounded by many lovely dogwoods in blossom, tall oaks, and several other kinds of trees. Except for the trees there was absolutely no planting. Not even a blade of grass had the courage to grow in the sand and gravel which was strewn about the new home. To make matters better, or worse, I had a frenzied urge to landscape the plot and little knowledge of how to proceed.

A pool entered into the mental scheme from the first.

I mention all this with the hope of reassuring those who, like myself, have the desire for a lovely garden and pool, but who lack the experience to make them.

Inexperience is always costly in time, patience, and money. I have paid the price in all three directions, but with experimentation and failure have come successes.

This book is written for the amateur gardener who has "the urge" to build a pool and seek simple, direct, and economical information.

The building of a pool may take a few hours or a few days. The planting may be done in the spring, but the joy of landscaping and developing a pool and its surroundings is never ending.

Plants and shrubs grow in size and acquire character with age. "New" rocks grow mossy and more colorful when placed near water. Each miniature ledge is a complete garden in itself and they may be treated in infinite variety when once the pool is built and the main plantings are established. There are many plants to be tried, and a wide variety of interesting aquatic life to swim, hop, and raise their young within its confines. The greatest thrill of all is the discovery of tiny pin-like goldfish which have somehow escaped the cannibalistic habits of their elders.

You will find that a pool attracts birds. I have noticed how readily the sound of trickling water brings them to my garden. If you will provide a shallow, pebbly place for the birds they will soon splash and bathe while you are sitting within a few feet of them. The shrubs and plants surrounding the water serve as a sanctuary for the feathered folk, while chipmunks scamper under the surrounding rocks.

The joy of your pool will begin the moment you plan it. If you do not mind a little clean soil on your hands and shoes, you will enjoy building it. Keep constantly before you a vision of the finished pool and the summer hours of leisure at the water's edge.

CHAPTER II

Where and How to Plan Your Pool

LOCATING the pool is the first and most important step in the building process. For instance, if your heart is set on having waterlilies in blossom, put your pool in a sunny place, or at least where the full sun will reach it most of the day. If your garden is shaded and graced by trees, make it a woodland pool and forget the lily blossoms. Lily pads will grow in the shade and are quite decorative.

This book is mainly about informal pools, because they are generally most satisfactory for the small place. There are situations, however, which suggest the more formal types. The character of its surroundings, amount of space available, proximity to buildings, and the natural "lay of the land" usually determine whether the formal or informal pool is most appropriate. For instance, if the pool is to be near the house, a porch, or other building, or is in a garden of straight lines or other geometric forms, the

formal or semi-formal pool is in keeping and
will best harmonize with its surroundings.

If the ground is uneven or there is opportunity to create sloping banks and little ledges,
by all means build the naturalistic water garden. Keep this type of pool as far away from
buildings as possible.

Each garden or plot will dictate or suggest a
different location and treatment. Sloping and
level ground are equally desirable. A level plot
may be made uneven by the excavated soil, logs,
and rocks. Uneven, hilly situations are not easily
leveled and should be made the most of. (See
Chapter IX, "Hillside Pools and Brooks.")

Usually the back corner of the garden with
its screening of trees and shrubs is the ideal
location. The pool may be the objective at the
end of the garden path. At the time of locating
it, plan the routes to it. The winding informal
path appropriately leads to the woodland pool,
while the straight walk terminates in more so-
phisticated surroundings (Figs. 2 and 3).

In general, the informal pool is more appropriate and offers greater interest for the average
small place. If you have trees and shrubs
already growing in a desirable location, by all
means use them for background.

The pool should be placed where it may be

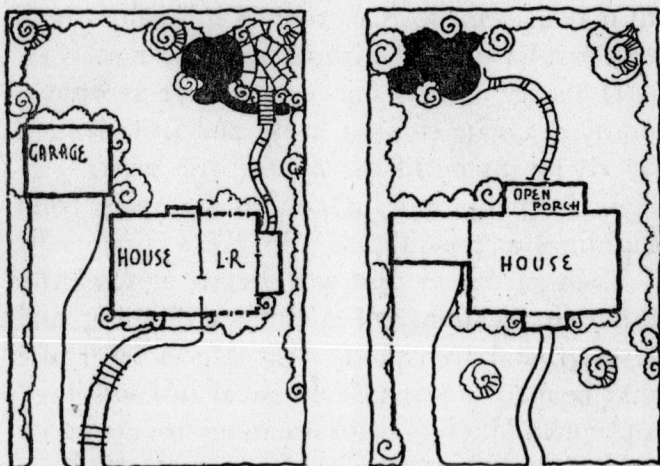

FIG. 2.   LOCATING THE INFORMAL POOL

Against a background of trees and shrubs but where it can be seen and enjoyed from living-room windows or porch, the small informal pool adds interest even to the smallest lot.

seen best from the porch or living-room windows. Think of the surface of the water as a huge mirror.

Use the garden hose or clothesline to make an outline on the ground. Simply lay the rope down loosely in the shape of a large irregular loop (Fig. 4). Study and adjust the enclosed shape.

The distant view of the "water mirror"

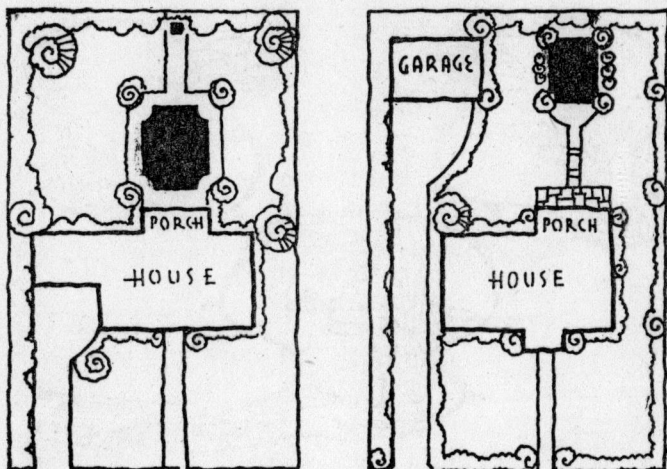

FIG. 3. LOCATING THE FORMAL POOL

Usually nearer the house and with balanced plantings about it, the formal or semi-formal pool should harmonize in its outlines with the rectangular lines of buildings and straight walks.

should be down its length. If you plan a view of the water's surface from the porch, have the longest dimension of the pool parallel with your line of sight from that point. Size is most important. Distance diminishes the area of a surface. For instance, a ten-foot pool at fifty feet appears to be less than half that size. Remember that plants growing at the water's edge will further cut down the surface view from a distance.

FIG. 4. INFORMAL POOLS OF IRREGULAR SHAPE

The best shape may be determined by laying down an irregular loop of rope or garden hose and studying it from various points of vantage.

After deciding on the size and shape of the water area, begin excavating at least six inches outside of the rope all around. The building material will take up this space (Fig. 7).

For more complete information on landscape planning for the small place see Doubleday Garden Handbook No. 4— HOW TO PLAN THE HOME LANDSCAPE, obtainable where you bought this Handbook.

CHAPTER III

How to Build the Pool

THE ideal time to build a pool is in the early spring. Do a little mental gardening during those trying weeks between winter and spring, and as soon as the frost is out of the ground lay the "rope plan" as described in Chapter II. Study this for a few days from various viewpoints: the upstairs windows, the porch, and from the living room.

To be specific, I am going to use my own pool as an example. It is approximately ten by ten feet, with a brook fifteen feet long. It has proven most satisfactory for the eighty by a hundred-and-twenty foot plot. I shall tell you how I built it. The drawings illustrate the planning and building of this pool.

CONSTRUCTION EXPERIENCE

As soon as the frost left the ground, we laid the plan and began excavating. The surroundings being flat, we decided to use the excavated

soil as a bank at the rear of the pool (Fig. 5).
Boards were laid on edge and supported by

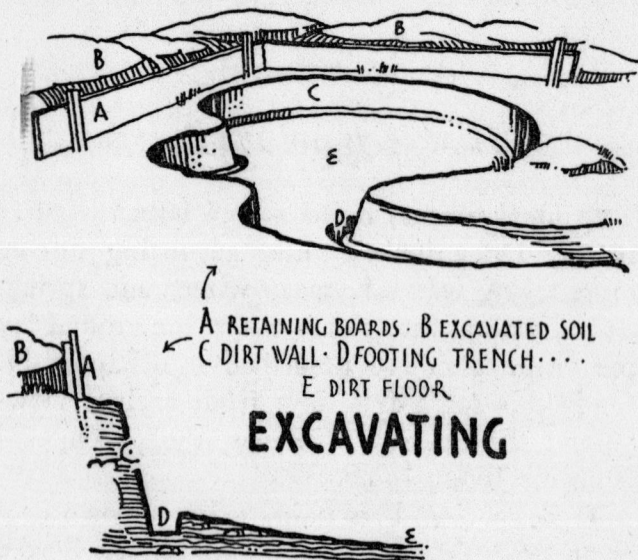

A RETAINING BOARDS · B EXCAVATED SOIL
C DIRT WALL · D FOOTING TRENCH · · · ·
E DIRT FLOOR

EXCAVATING

FIG. 5.   THE FIRST STEP IN BUILDING THE POOL

Dig at least six inches outside the finished size and eight
inches deeper than the finished depth to allow for concrete
sides and bottom.

stakes to retain the dirt pile and to prevent it
being scattered about.

Below the top surface the soil is generally
poor. Mine was mostly sand. To richen this for
future use, I alternated a layer of dry leaves

with a layer of soil as it was piled. The leaves were gathered from among the shrubs where they had drifted the preceding fall. More about soil later.

It was planned to have the water twelve inches deep at the sides, and about two feet deep in the center. Building material, cinders, and concrete were to be approximately eight inches thick on the bottom, so it was necessary to excavate to about twenty inches at the edges and thirty-two inches in the center. All around the sides a footing trench was dug about six inches wide and four inches deep as shown in Fig. 5D.

At this point we considered drainage. A drain-well is desirable but not necessary if there is a near-by slope away from the pool or if the drain in the cellar floor can be reached from the pool by a length of garden hose. In either case the water may be siphoned out of the pool, it being only necessary to have the draining end of the hose lower than the bottom of the pool.

A well-balanced pool need be emptied only once or twice a year.

DRAIN-WELLS

Presuming that a drain-well is necessary, it should be excavated and piped before the concrete goes into the pool walls (Fig. 6). Do not build the drain-well under the pool as it will be inaccessible and weaken the foundation. Excavate a little to one side.

The drain-well may be constructed in various ways and of different materials. A large empty tar barrel, set open-end down, is good. Any large, firm oak barrel, creosoted inside and out, is quite satisfactory. Cresote stain is inexpensive and may be purchased at hardware stores. Large chimney flue tiles, two or more set side by side on end in the ground, are more lasting and perhaps easier to obtain from building-supply houses. Cesspool blocks are made especially for this purpose and are easily built up. Brick or stone may be used, but in all cases lay up the walls with a minimum of concrete, allowing plenty of escape spaces for the water.

As to the size of the drain-well; this depends on the quantity of water to be drained and the porosity of the soil surrounding it. A drain-well set in hardpan will be extremely slow, so every effort should be made to reach sand or porous earth.

For a ten-by-ten-foot pool, one large barrel or two large chimney flues, or the equivalent, is enough.

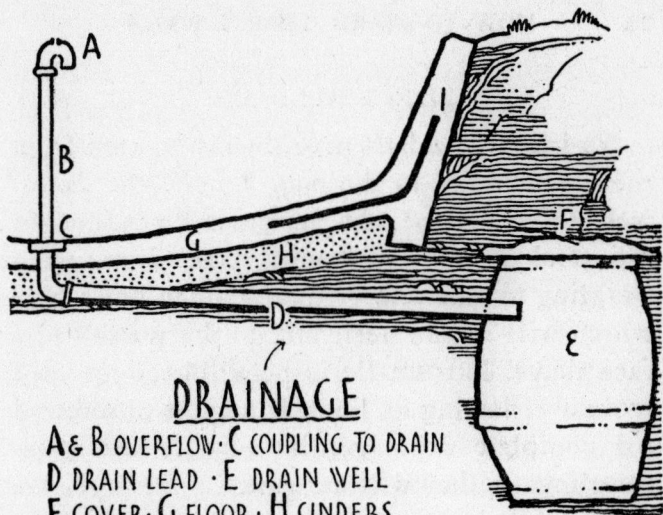

DRAINAGE

A & B OVERFLOW · C COUPLING TO DRAIN
D DRAIN LEAD · E DRAIN WELL
F COVER · G FLOOR · H CINDERS
I REINFORCEMENT ·

← CHIMNEY TILES FOR
DRAIN WELL · A-LEAD
B-BROKEN SPACE FOR
CONNECTION

WATER SUPPLY

A- HOSE CONNECTION
B- HOUSE
C- CONTROL TO POOL
D- OUTLET TO POOL

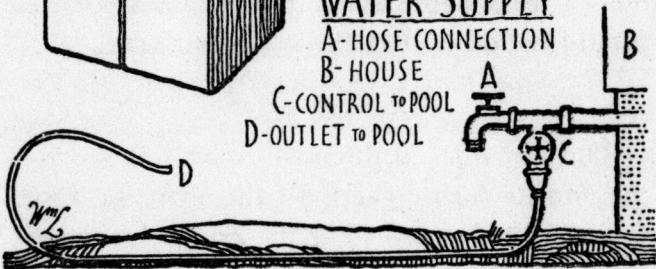

FIG. 6.   DRAINAGE AND WATER SUPPLY

23

PIPING THE DRAIN

An inch-and-a-half pipe should be used from the lowest point in the pool floor to the drain-well (Fig. 6, top). At the inner floor level of the pool this pipe should have a reducing coupling to take a three-quarter-inch brass pipe which will extend vertically to the water's surface above. This smaller pipe will keep the pool from overflowing its sides. It may be unscrewed for complete drainage. Be sure to use brass couplings as they will not rust.

When the connecting drain pipe is in place, cover the drain-well opening with a slab of stone or concrete. Boards will not do as they will soon rot and cave in. When the cover is in place, the hole above may be filled. If planting is planned over the drain-well, it is desirable to have the top two feet or more below the surface. This is reasonable as the top of the drain-well should be lower than the pool floor level.

CONCRETE FORMS

The dirt sides of the pool excavation serve as the outside form to support the concrete. Inner forms are to be used (Fig. 7). For the geometric shape, boards are satisfactory, but are not flexible enough for the irregular sides of the informal pool.

Heavy tarred roofing material which comes in rolls is good for the purpose. Old linoleum, roofing tin, or other material which is inexpensive and pliable may be used. The material should be cut in long strips a little wider than the side depths of the excavation. For instance, if the excavation is twenty-four inches deep at the edges for a pool to be twelve inches deep, the material will be cut in strips thirty inches wide.

It is safer to coat the concrete side of all forms with heavy grease.

At this point, many flat-sided stakes about three feet long will be needed. Sharpened boards from packing boxes are ideal as their flat sides offer good support for the roofing paper. You will also need a quantity of blocks or short pieces of wood six inches long. These will be used between the form and the dirt sides to keep the space open for concrete.

Stand the roofing paper on edge in the footing trench. Drive stakes inside it not more than six inches apart to prevent the weight of the concrete bulging the form (Fig. 7). The small blocks should be used between roofing paper and dirt walls as needed. Tacks through the paper into the blocks will hold them in place.

Most important, do not fail to remove all blocks as the concrete is poured, as they will cause the pool to leak if left in place.

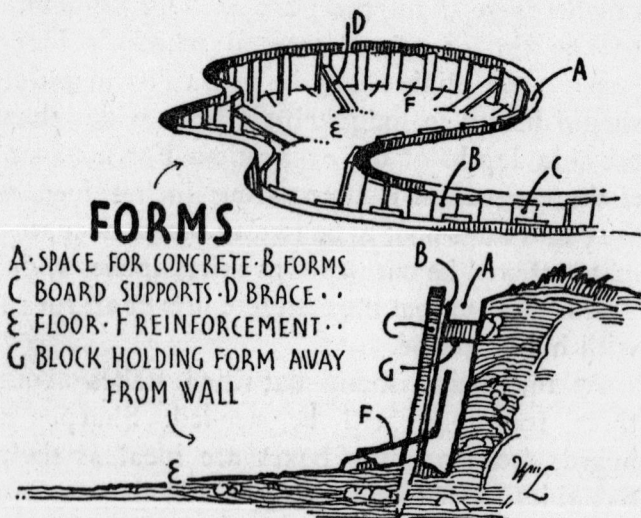

FORMS

A·SPACE FOR CONCRETE·B FORMS
C BOARD SUPPORTS·D BRACE··
E FLOOR· F REINFORCEMENT··
G BLOCK HOLDING FORM AWAY
FROM WALL

FIG. 7.   HOW TO SET THE FORMS

Six inches or more inside the dirt walls flexible forms to hold the concrete are held in place by wooden blocks and stakes.

REINFORCEMENT

Reinforcement between the side walls and the floor is desirable.

For reinforcement use fencing wire, iron pipe, metal strips, or other similar material, old or new. It is necessary to cast one end of the wire into the side wall leaving the other free to be imbedded into the floor when it is poured. Be particularly careful to reinforce pools which have angular corners.

MIXING CONCRETE

Concrete is made of Portland cement, clean sand, and gravel. A safe formula is: one part cement, two parts sharp, clean sand, three parts of clean half-inch gravel or crushed stone.

When informed of the area, depth, and thickness of concrete in your pool, your local dealer in building materials will estimate and supply the right quantities. All of this material should be trucked as near the excavation as possible.

The side walls should be completed in a day, as an interruption in the process may cause weakness. If it is not possible to finish the walls in one operation, insert some mesh wire or reinforcement in the wet concrete and allow several inches of it to protrude as a binder for the next day's material.

The cement may be mixed on the concrete garage floor, or in a large shallow box made especially for the purpose (Fig. 8). A floor surface at least six by six feet will be needed. The box with its sides may be three feet by six feet by a foot deep. It should be strongly and tightly

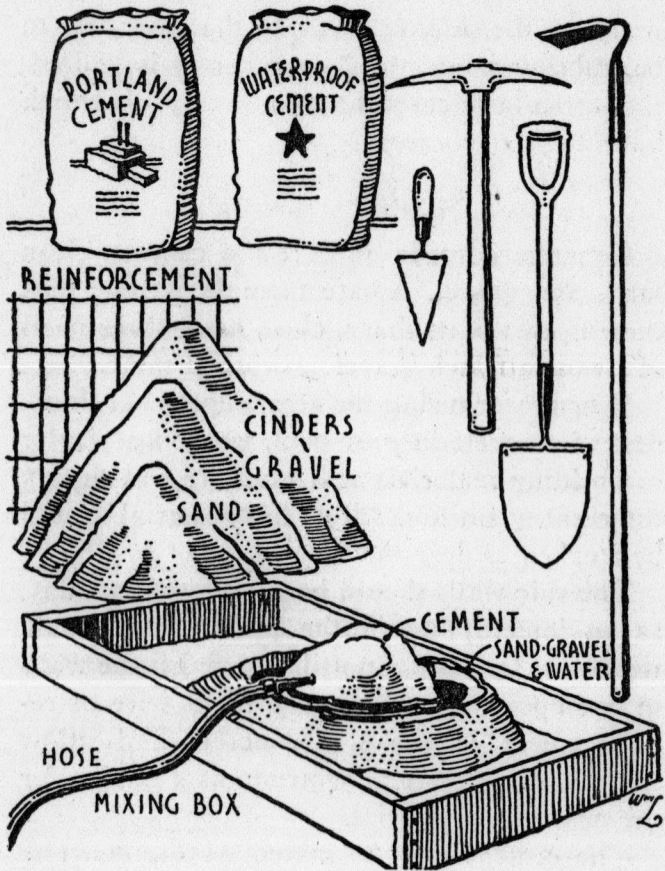

FIG. 8. CONSTRUCTION TOOLS AND MATERIALS

Consult your building-supply dealer as to quantities of cement, sand, and gravel required for a one-two-three mix, giving him the dimensions of your pool.

made of inch boards. The advantage of a box is that it may be used right at the pool site.

A hose or source of water supply should be handy. Now begin measuring, using a shovel as a measure. Remember, for each full shovel of cement there will be two of sand and three of gravel. A convenient batch is ten shovels of sand, fifteen of gravel, and five of cement. First alternate two shovels of sand with three of gravel until twenty-five shovels in all of this material is piled together in your mixing box. Hollow out a space in the top of this pile of sand and gravel and measure into it five shovels of cement. Turn all over repeatedly with the shovel and hoe until the dry cement is thoroughly mixed with the other ingredients. Now hollow the top of the pile again, and add water, mixing it in as rapidly as it will be absorbed. Hoe all back and forth until the mixture is of a thick, though runny, consistency.

Fresh concrete should be washed clean from the floor and tools by using a strong stream from the hose. This should be done before the mixture begins to harden.

POURING THE POOL

Now you are ready to fill the forms. Shovel the concrete between the roofing paper and the earth wall (Fig. 7). Tamp it well into place with a long stick, and remove all blocks as you fill up to them. Repeat the process until all side-wall forms are filled.

As the top begins to set, bevel it back from the pool as illustrated in Fig. 6 (top), and smooth the surface. This back bevel will help prevent surface water from flowing into the finished pool.

Forms may be removed from the side walls as soon as the concrete has set. This usually takes from twelve to twenty-four hours, depending on atmospheric conditions. Carefully remove the stakes and the roofing paper. Rough edges may be smoothed by rubbing with the flat surface of a brick.

To finish the bottom, proceed as follows: Spread a layer of cinders or crushed stone to a depth of four inches over the entire dirt floor of the pool. This will preclude heaving by the frost. Mix the concrete as before and lay it evenly to a depth of six to eight inches, imbedding the corner reinforcements into it as in Fig. 6 (top). Begin at one side wall and proceed toward the other, being absolutely certain that the mixture is thoroughly tamped against these walls to insure a fusion. Slightly round the bottom into the side walls to strengthen the angle between floor and wall. Smooth the surface with a trowel, and lastly, by brushing with a damp, stiff, old broom.

In the course of concreting the bottom, the drain pipe will be adjusted at level of the lowest point of the floor. This should be carefully arranged, as illustrated in Fig. 6 (top), to insure complete drainage when the pool is cleaned.

WATERPROOFING

As further insurance against leakage, I suggest an inch of rich concrete over the entire inner surface to waterproof the pool. This is mixed one shovel of cement to one of sand, with as little water as possible.

The mixture should be stiff so as to cling to the pool walls. Apply it with a trowel, and lastly, before it has set, smooth the entire inner surface with the stiff, damp, old broom.

The basin of the pool is finished (Fig. 9), but it is wise not to walk in it or fill it with water for at least three days.

THE WATER SUPPLY

The garden hose is as useful in filling the pool as it is in emptying it. No special pipe is necessary. However, I feel that a copper tube from the house to the pool is well worth the

little labor and expense it takes to connect and
lay it. The sight and sound of trickling water is
one of the delights of the water garden.

The labor necessary to pipe water to a pool is
usually very little. If there is a hose connection
at the foundation of the house near by, it will

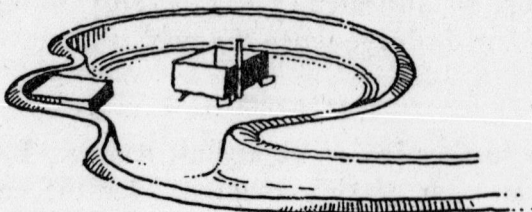

FIG. 9.   THE POOL IS POURED

Here the forms have been removed, the top edges and
bottom finished, and boxes for waterlilies and bog plants are
in place. Fig. 20 shows the same pool with the landscaping
done.

serve your purpose. Remove the single faucet
and apply a double one, one for the hose and
another for the pool (Fig. 6, bottom).

If there is no hose outlet on the nearest side
of the house, it will be necessary to carry a
water pipe from the cellar through the house
foundation. This is a small job for a plumber.

Quarter or half-inch copper tubing is the
most desirable connection between house and
pool. It is reasonable in cost, flexible to handle,

and will stand freezing which might burst ordinary pipe. Either a threaded coupling or a tight joint made with tire tape may connect the tubing to the house faucet. The tubing will be laid on the ground leading by the shortest route to the back of the pool. You should have several feet to spare because it is hardly possible to decide on the exact point of outlet until the pool is landscaped. If feasible, it is desirable to have the outlet several feet above and back of the pool so the water may cascade into it.

Mark the ground along the tube and dig a trench about twelve inches deep. Lay the tubing into this trench and replace the soil. In the late fall, before freezing, the house end may be disconnected and the tube blown clear of water either by "lung power" or with an automobile pump.

Many plans call for a water valve near the pool, frequently in a box below the ground. Locating the valve at the house end has many advantages. First, it eliminates the labor and expense of a special connection. Secondly, it is much more attractive to have the water running as you and your visitors approach the pool. If the valve is located at the foundation of the house and hidden in the shrubbery, a quick turn of the wrist starts the water much more conveniently than stooping over a sunken valve box.

Large volume of water is not as desirable as a slight trickle or drip. The tiny stream is much more economical and its high-keyed tune more delightful than the gushing, larger stream. Rapid filling, like rapid emptying, may be accomplished with the garden hose.

A steady flow of water is not necessary. In fact, if lilies are to be grown, cold, running water is actually detrimental to their growth. It is delightful to have the sound and sight of trickling water while loitering about the pool or working in the garden. If properly balanced, there is no necessity for further circulation.

The formal pool sometimes calls for a vertical spray. The end of the tubing may be pinched together with pliers or a garden hose nozzle may be attached.

Where water is scarce or very costly, a small motor may be installed to use the same water over and over again. It is wise to consult a local plumber if such equipment is desired.

PROVISION FOR BOG PLANTS

Any pocket or area of soil a few inches deep, just under the surface of the water, is satisfactory for bog plants.

In building the pool, thought should be given to the plants which grow with only their feet in the water. A shallow box two feet by three feet by six inches deep may be used and camouflaged, or a definite place may be built of concrete in the pool. A shallow little box may be cut off under water by concreting a few large stones across a neck. Pockets for soil may be built up along the edges of stone and concrete (see Chapter VIII).

The walls and bottom of all pools, however, should be an unbroken mass of concrete. Do not cast in stones or other material for a rustic effect unless you care to run the risk of leakage. Many stones are porous. A stationary rough interior is most troublesome when the pool is cleaned. Do the rock work after the main basin is completed. At this time stone pockets and overhangs may be cemented into place.

CHAPTER IV

Small Informal Pools, Lily Tubs, and Bird Baths

MANY gardeners are deterred from building pools by the thought that extensive space is required and that considerable labor and expense are involved. Like a small garden, a tiny pool may have gem-like beauty.

I strongly advocate a garden of a size which is comparable to the time the owner can afford to give it. Better the little garden well planned and cared for than the extensive one ill kept. Save yourself worry and regret by planning your garden and its pool in proportion to the time you can devote to it.

Logically, the small garden offers limited space for a pool, and furthermore the scale of the pool and planting should be in keeping with its surroundings. A large piece of furniture seems to diminish the size of a room. The same rule applies to pools and gardens.

I like to think of the little informal pool as

a natural spring in the forest or field, a tiny basin set in rocks, ferns, and moss (Figs. 11 and 13). You will find one of these miniature pools desirable as a dipping place for the watering can, and the birds will be grateful, especially during the late summer months when water is hard for them to find.

BUILDING THE SMALL POOL

To build such a woodland spring or miniature pool, select a location against tall shrubs, under hemlocks, or under elderberry bushes. Scoop out a basin-like space in the ground (Fig. 10) to a size and depth desired. In climates where there is freezing and thawing, it is wise to provide a six- or eight-inch foundation of cinders or crushed stone to preclude heaving by the frost. Allowance must be made for this extra material at the time of excavating.

No forms are necessary as the earth sides and cinders will act as support. The sides below the ground level will not be steep enough to necessitate forms.

Mix the concrete: one part cement, two parts sharp, clean sand, and three parts half-inch gravel or crushed stone. For a small pool of this sort a bag or two of cement is ample. Mix the concrete thoroughly as suggested in Chapter

III. Keep the mixture stiff rather than too moist, so it will hold its desired form when applied as the inside wall. Build the wall to the same level all around except where the overflow

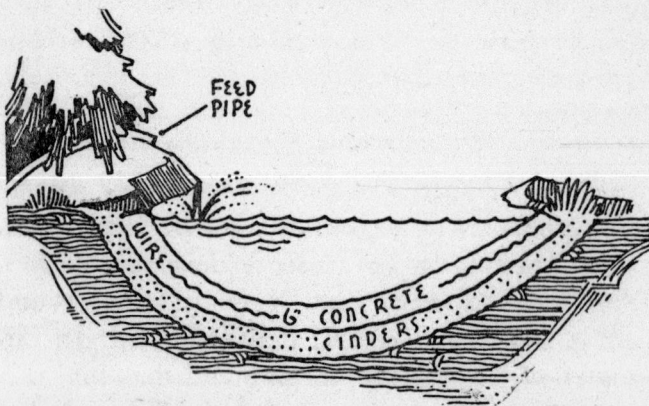

FIG. 10. A SMALL POOL BUILT WITHOUT FORMS

A basin scooped in the ground is lined with concrete laid on cinders, with wire reinforcement.

is wanted. Pools *have* been built which overflowed in unexpected directions!

It is hardly necessary to have a drain-well for such a small basin. The water may be allowed to overflow into the surrounding soil for bog plants. There is some danger of the overflow undermining the ground beneath the pool. It is safest to set a short length of pipe (about three

feet by one inch) horizontally into the concrete
wall at the desired water level. At the outlet
end, dig a hole and throw in a wheelbarrow
load or two of broken stones or bricks. A small
piece of copper mesh wire over the intake end
will keep fish from trying to squeeze through.
If a running water supply is desired, build it as
described in Chapter III.

REINFORCEMENT

In severe climates it is recommended that
even small pools be reinforced. Heavy fence
wire, iron rods, or similar material may be
woven together to form a lining for the excavation. As the concrete is poured, this mesh may
be adjusted to the center of the mixture by
supporting it on small stones.

Cracked pools cannot be permanently
mended. It is economy to do the job correctly
for once and all.

"Cure" the concrete for three days by keeping
it damp with moist leaves or hay. Fill and
empty five times during the following two
weeks.

Landscaping may be done in the meantime.
Proceed the same as described in Chapter VI
except on a smaller scale (Fig. 11). Large
stones, plants, and accessories will diminish the

size of the already small pool. Keep its surroundings small and relative in scale, much the

BOG
OVERFLOW

FIG. 11.   THE SMALL POOL FINISHED

Naturalistic planting of the pool shown in Fig. 10. See
also Chapter VI.

same as one does in arranging a "Japanese" dish
garden.

TUB OR BARREL POOLS

A perfectly satisfactory and extremely simple
lily pool may be constructed by using a large

wash tub or a half barrel (Fig. 12). An empty
oil barrel sawed in half, burned out by lighting
newspaper in it, is quite satisfactory. The receptacle used should be well constructed and of
hard wood.

FIG. 12. A TUB POOL FOR WATERLILIES

Plant in soil in a tub or half barrel sunk in the ground in
the sun.

Such a pool may be set into the ground or
even fully exposed in a suitable place. If lilies
are desired, full sun is necessary. Such a tub
garden will accommodate one of many varieties
of lilies and is quite satisfactory where time,
space, and money must be saved. Filling and

emptying such a pool may be accomplished easily with the garden hose.

Only very low-growing plants should be planted close to the tub garden. The surroundings may be landscaped as illustrated in Fig. 13.

FIG. 13.   THE TUB POOL LANDSCAPED

Rocks and a few low-growing plants make an attractive pool garden of the simple tub shown in Fig. 12.

BIRD BATHS

The bird bath is the smallest sort of pool, though not the least important. Every pool should have provision for birds. They require but a small area of clean, shallow water. An

inch or two of depth with a gravel bottom, and
a near-by perch in the form of an overhanging
limb or shrubs completely satisfies the needs of
the feathered folks. They are fond of dipping
and splashing and then flitting to a convenient
perch to preen and dry their feathers.

The safest bath for birds is set on a pedestal
or above the ground level apart from dense
shrubbery or other hiding places for the wait-
ing cat. A cat soon learns the habits of birds and
will stalk them as they bathe.

If the bath is near shrubbery, set a strip of
coarse-mesh chicken wire vertically just inside
the planting in such a manner as to prevent the
cat from springing on the birds. Prowling, bird-
killing cats should be destroyed.

Inexpensive pedestal bird baths may be
bought, appropriately located, and planted with
a few iris or low shrubs at their base. It is
hardly economy in time or money to build a
bird bath of this type.

A few suggestions for the ground-level basin
are appropriate. The simplest way to construct
such a tiny pool is to hollow out a shallow place
in the ground and concrete it as suggested for
the small informal pool. While there is danger
of winter breakage making reinforcement desirable, it is not necessary. A pool of this kind

can be so quickly and inexpensively built that elaborate processes are not called for. The concrete need be only three or four inches thick to prevent leakage. The safest to use is waterproof cement. A bag of this cement will be more than enough.

Remember to keep the water very shallow at one side and gradually deepen it to five or six inches at the center or back. A few pebbles and small plants complete the scheme.

The top of a metal ash barrel, a large wooden chopping bowl, a broad shallow piece of pottery, or other receptacle may be used. Set any one of these into the ground and fill with water and pebbles.

All shallow, still water should be changed or flushed once a week to discourage mosquitoes, which are likely to breed in such places.

CHAPTER V

Building Formal or Geometric Pools

CHAPTER II suggests where formal pools are appropriate. Read that again before you decide to make your new pool a formal one.

You have decided on a formal or geometric design! This type of pool is usually the easiest to construct. The simplest plan is a square or rectangle which requires only a box-like form.

Much more interesting and individual pools may be built by varying the shape from these two forms. Various designs are suggested in Fig. 14.

CONSTRUCTION

Using a rope or hose as suggested in Chapter II, lay out the plan of your pool on the ground. Its sides should run parallel with or at right angles to building lines, paths, terraces, or walls. Consider the intended approach or view most carefully and place the pool in proper relation to it.

Begin the excavation six inches outside of the rope plan, keeping the earth walls vertical and firm to act as the outside form. Plan the drain

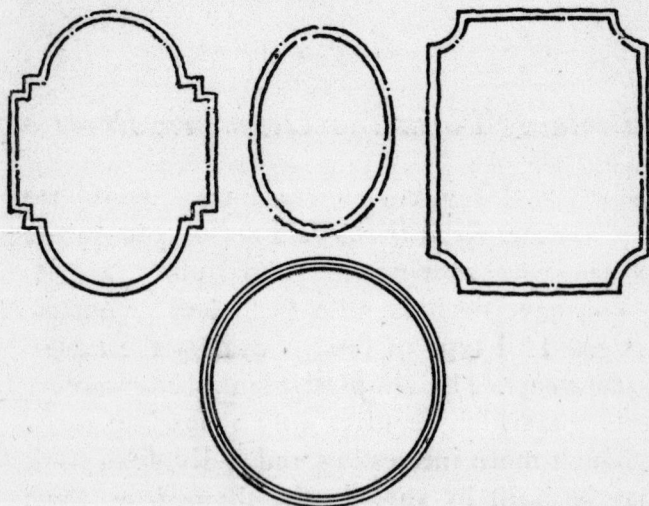

FIG. 14. APPROPRIATE SHAPES FOR FORMAL POOLS

Rectangles are easiest to construct, but circles and other regular geometric designs may also fit appropriately into formal and semi-formal surroundings.

and overflow pipe as suggested in Chapter III. Build the inside form solidly of one- by six-inch boards and framing material, with one-by-two-inch stakes (Fig. 15). The board form should be about six inches away from the earth sides and concrete is poured into this space. It is best

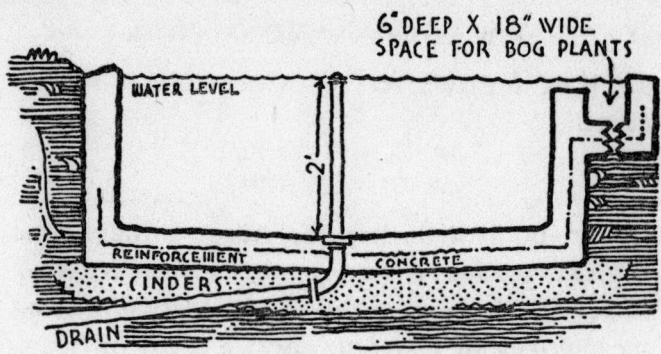

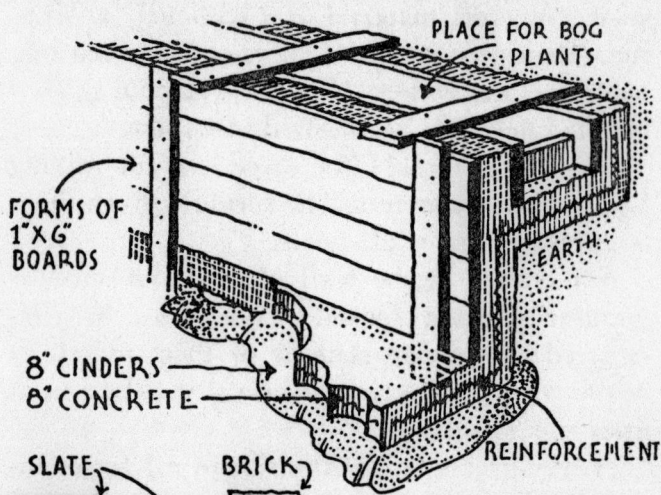

6" DEEP X 18" WIDE SPACE FOR BOG PLANTS

WATER LEVEL

2'

REINFORCEMENT

CINDERS

CONCRETE

DRAIN

PLACE FOR BOG PLANTS

FORMS OF 1"X6" BOARDS

EARTH

8" CINDERS
8" CONCRETE

REINFORCEMENT

SLATE

BRICK

WAYS TO FINISH THE TOP

FORMAL POOLS

Fig. 15. Constructing and Finishing the Rim

to allow for two feet of water at the deepest
point.

REINFORCEMENT

The pool with straight sides, corners, and
angles demands reinforcement. Corners are weak
under the pressure of freezing. Before or during
the pouring of concrete insert a mesh of heavy
wire (fencing material is excellent) or iron
rods. Bend this around corners and between side
walls and the bottom (Fig. 15). A pool so constructed need not be emptied in winter.

Read Chapter III for directions for mixing
and applying concrete. The formula given there
is appropriate for all pools.

For curves in the wall of the pool and for
circular pools a special frame must be constructed of wooden slats or of sheet metal, or
heavy roofing material will do if it is braced at
intervals (Fig. 16).

Heavy grease on the interior of all forms in-
sures their easy removal when concrete has set.
Forms may be carefully removed in twenty-
four to forty-eight hours. Cure the drying concrete for a few days by a light sprinkling each
evening, or better still by a covering of burlap
bags or straw kept damp.

Fill and empty the pool several times in the

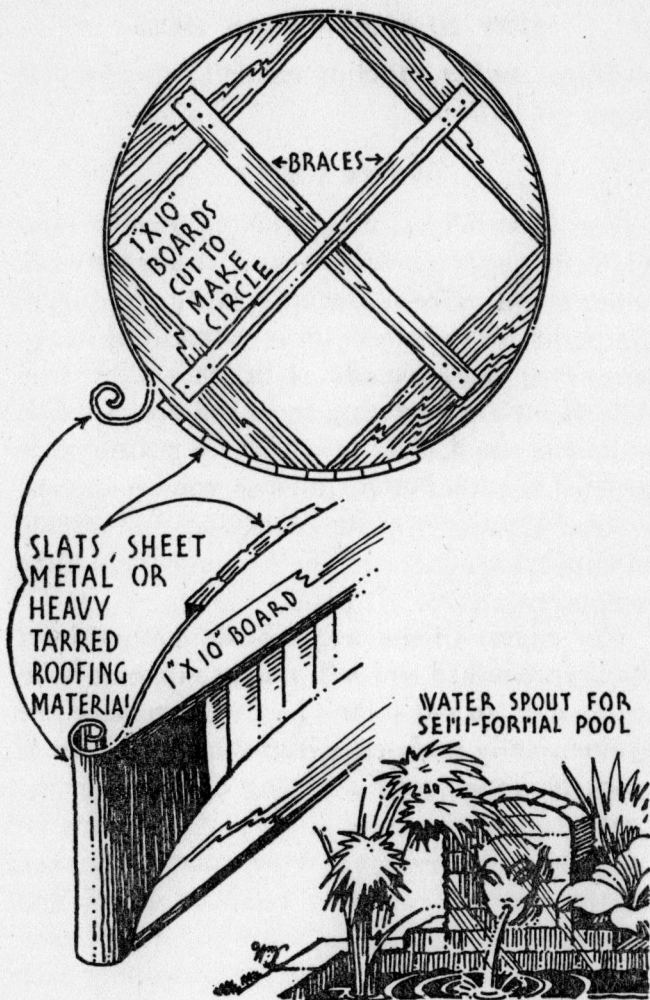

BRACES

1"X 10" BOARDS CUT TO MAKE CIRCLE

SLATS, SHEET METAL OR HEAVY TARRED ROOFING MATERIAL

1"X 10" BOARD

WATER SPOUT FOR SEMI-FORMAL POOL

FIG. 16. BUILDING CIRCULAR FORMS

first two weeks to eliminate alkali, which is injurious to fish.

WATER SUPPLY

The formal pool may be filled and emptied with the garden hose or piped as suggested in Chapter III. I recommend a piped water supply, either as a vertical spray which drops back into the pool at one end or in the center, or as a jet of water emanating from a piece of sculpture at one end of the pool or from a niche in a wall (Fig. 16, bottom). The formal pool calls for a conventional water supply.

FINISHING THE COPING

The edges of the concrete at the ground level may be smoothed and left plain, or covered with brick, slate, or cut stone (Fig. 15, bottom). The geometrically set border is most appropriate. A brick house suggests a coping of brick on the near-by pool.

CHAPTER VI

Landscaping the Informal Pool-side

LET us assume that the basin of the pool is
complete. Several days are needed for the concrete to cure or slowly dry. During the following two weeks the pool should be filled and
emptied five times to remove the alkali from
the concrete. You need not be idle during this
time. In fact, this is just the opportunity to ar-
range the rock work, the soil, shrubs, and water-
side plants. The naturalistic and the formal
pool differ greatly in their landscape treatment.
We shall consider the informal problem first.

GRADING

The informal pool suggests irregular, natural
treatment in its grading and general landscaping. If the pool has been built against large trees
or an established background these will dictate
the grades and arrangement to some extent.

From the very beginning, you should know
the finished effect you want. This may come
from your own rough sketch, perhaps suggested

by illustrations in this book, or from clippings
from garden magazines. No art ability is required to make a rough sketch of your idea.
Simply use a large piece of cardboard or paper
and draw with a crayon or soft black pencil a
plan and elevation of your pool, indicating the
plants as in Fig. 17. Merely groupings and plan
are wanted, not detailed drawings of the rocks
and plants.

Better than all other references is Nature's
pool. Visit and observe any natural pools in
your vicinity. Notice especially the way rocks,
logs, moss, and little plants combine and blend
into a harmonious whole. No one is more important than the combination. While I do not
suggest tearing apart and ruining the beauty
spots of the countryside, I see no reason why
certain details of wood or field pools should not
be carefully moved and preserved in your own
garden. Most certainly you should not leave an
ugly gash of soil in moving rocks and plants.
Fill in the spot with sod or near-by material
to help Nature cover the scar.

KINDS OF ROCK

Rocks, logs, or stumps are highly desirable
to use in grading about the natural pool. They

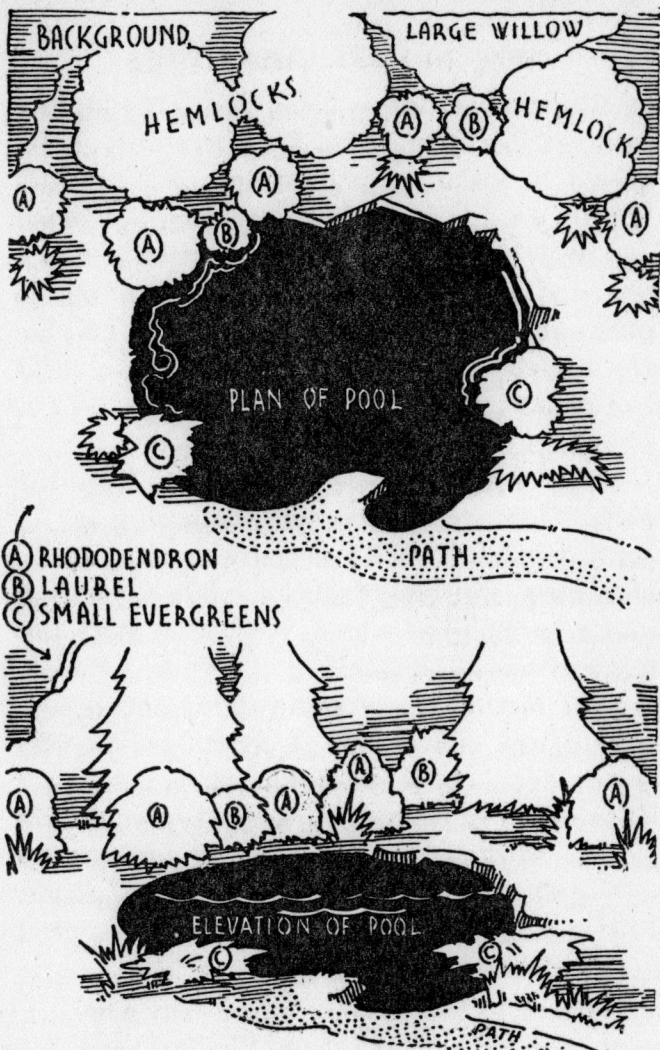

FIG. 17. HOW TO PLAN YOUR PLANTINGS

Before you start grading or placing rocks make a rough sketch, blocking in shapes and sizes of rocks and plants.

have a tangible defining character which is a relief for the soft contours of soil and plants. They may be made to overhang, to jut out and build up in a way impossible with any other material. If rock is not available, use rough logs laid horizontally as they are frequently found in the woods, partially covered with leaves, mosses, and vines.

Any rock except cobbles may be used. The best for plants, and often seen in model gardens, is gray, pitted limestone, or coral formation. Unless one lives where this material occurs naturally, however, the cost of transportation makes it prohibitive. Ledge, or stratified rock is excellent. If it is available in your neighborhood by all means use it.

Foreign-looking, "imported" rock usually looks out of place in the small garden. Use the material nearest at hand for the most natural effect. A Long Island Czechoslovakian cesspool contractor frequently offers me excellent stone and amusement by delivering "two-thousand-year-old rock" which he finds in excavating. To him, all twisted or crooked stone is very old, while a plain cobble is comparatively new. Let your pool-side be landscaped with "very antique" rocks.

KINDS OF SOIL

In Chapter III we suggested using the excavated soil in grading the pool-side. This may be done if enough really good soil is available. Too often the good soil is only a few inches deep, and then one strikes sand, clay, and poorer kinds.

Top-soil is usually expensive, so economy suggests preparing it. Poorer soils may be mixed with old straw-filled manure, peat moss, dead leaves or compost to supply organic, slow-rotting material—humus. Chemical fertilizers give plant foods but have no leavening qualities.

Woods-plants, evergreens, laurel, and rhododendrons need no other fertilizer than this compost mixture.

Either before the grading process or when the soil is being placed, prepare it thoroughly for permanent satisfaction to yourself and the growing things dependent on it.

PLACING OF ROCKS AND SOIL

The comedy of American gardening is in its countless so-called rock gardens. They might be called "gas station" rock gardens for they frequently are found as part of the typical

American gasoline or roadside stand. Nature never sets sharp, jagged rocks evenly on end or at regular intervals.

FIG. 18. HOW TO PLACE THE ROCKS

Begin at the edge of the pool and work away from it, setting the rocks firmly on their largest bases, more or less in strata or ledges as they appear in nature, but tilted into the soil to conserve moisture for plants and prevent washing. Fig. 1 shows how these same rocks were planted.

A ledge-like or flat arrangement of rocks is best (Fig. 18). Begin at the edge of the pool and work away from it, using soil and stone alternately. Allow some rocks to overhang the

concrete edge, but do not place these in a neck-
lace-like regular ring all around the edge. At
least half of each stone will be embedded in the
earth for permanency and best appearance, with
the largest base at the bottom.

Surface-water drainage away from the pool is
extremely important, and especially difficult
until plants have become established in the new
loose soil. Provision should be made for the
sudden heavy shower when the rain does not
have time to soak into the ground. Rocks should
be tilted back with exposed edges slightly
higher than the submerged ones. This will re-
tard the drainage into the pool and divert
necessary moisture to the deeper earth.

Those trained in design know that garden
making is distinctly a design problem, and that
the rules of design apply to it. One of the first
rules for an interesting design is variety with
coördination. For instance, group your rocks
into one large ledge, then an open space for soil
and low plants, and then a smaller rock group.
The strata or "lay" of the rocks will be the same
throughout, and this will insure coördination.
In other words, if all rocks are laid horizontally
they will appear to be outcroppings of the same
ledge (Fig. 18).

Avoid stones on edge and gullies leading from higher ground to the pool below (Fig. 19) as they are water channels. Such gullies may be blocked by a minor outcropping of rock at the

FIG. 19.   HOW NOT TO PLACE ROCKS

Nature never plants rocks on end nor at regular intervals. Such an arrangement has spoiled many a pool planting.

top and again part way down. If many rocks are used near the pool, place an occasional outcropping some distance from it further to tie in the arrangement. Deep soil must be provided for the larger plants, while sedums and many other small plants grow well in cracks and crannies between the stones.

You should constantly keep planting in mind.

Leave adequate space to save the labor of moving stone during the planting process.

A thorough watering-down of the grading and rock work will help settle it and will show you where surface-water runs are likely to develop. After this you are ready for planting, the next stage of the fascinating job of garden making.

PLANTING THE POOL-SITE

If your main object is to grow waterlilies, you should avoid the shade of large trees and shrubs. This does not mean the pool must be a barren puddle in the center of a lawn. Trees and taller shrubs should be planted in a group or bank on one side only, allowing full sunlight access to the remaining three sides. Some background is highly recommended to give character, mystery, and variety to the pool. Fish are fond of the shade cast by branches hanging low over the water's edge.

In exposed places a windbreak is indispensable as a protection for waterlilies. White or silver birches and weeping willows offer a maximum of beauty and a minimum of shade. These are graceful, lacy, rapid-growing trees.

In front of the taller trees plant evergreens, especially the hemlock, which may be a little more expensive than other common varieties of evergreens, but its lasting beauty and appropriateness are worth the difference in price. A group of three hemlocks six feet high, planted five or six feet apart, will be effective. In front of the hemlocks plant mountain laurel or rhododendron. These broad-leaf evergreens are a beautiful contrast against the fine sprays of the hemlocks.

The object in the planting is to create a series of irregular steps from the water's edge to the rocks, to the low plants, to the shrubs, the evergreens, and then to the tallest trees (Figs. 1, 11, and 20).

Each pool and its locality will present a different problem. For instance, the best plants for New York may not be procurable in Texas. Give careful consideration to native plantings, the things growing wild in your vicinity. They are economical and are most likely to thrive. It is logical to consult your local nurseryman.

In planning the use of larger trees and shrubs one should think of their mature size and not plant too closely. As a rule, new planting "stands still" the first year while it is adjusting itself and making new root growth. It should be well watered during this time. During the second year, new shoots and foliage spring out and make surprising growth.

FIG. 20.   HOW TO PLANT YOUR POOL

Plant not too closely but as nearly as possible as Nature does it—smaller plants near the water, grading back irregularly to the shrubs and trees in the background. This is the same pool of which construction is shown in Figs. 4, 5, 7, and 9. See also Figs. 1 and 11.

Before planting a single new shrub it is wise to place a number of tall and short stakes designating the location of principal pieces. These will be useful along with your rough elevation sketch such as is suggested in Fig. 17.

As a rule, nursery-grown stock is more easily moved than plants which grow wild. In the nursery you will find the better specimens of tried shrubs which have developed a compact root system through transplanting and root pruning. Reliable nurseries guarantee their stock as true to name, offer advice, and many will plant your purchases on delivery. Go to the nursery yourself and select the specimens you want. Frequently a crooked, picturesque plant is more desirable than a perfectly symmetrical one.

The cost and your location may make it convenient to use some gathered material. Many plants are easily moved and require little care, but usually it pays to do the job correctly to preclude a setback in growth.

For most things, early spring and fall are the proper moving seasons. If a deciduous tree is moved when in foliage, take a larger earth ball, trim branches drastically, and keep well watered for the next twelve months.

SHRUBS AND PLANTS

The common elderberry is one of the most satisfactory pool-side shrubs. It is easy to move, grows rapidly, and may be controlled by trimming. In June it has great masses of white blossoms which later develop into clusters of rich, dark berries. Flowering quince is ornamental. Select the crooked bush rather than the straight tree variety. Where tall, upright evergreens are desired, cedars are recommended, but do not plant them in dense shade as they thrive best in sunlight. The dogwood has a drooping umbrella shape which is graceful and beautiful. Before the leaves, it has drifts of white blossoms. The clean dense foliage is followed by bright red berries liked by the birds and squirrels.

Select smaller shrubs, both evergreen and deciduous, for variety of form and color. For instance, the broad-leaf evergreens should be contrasted with those of finer foliage, such as yew, juniper, and arborvitæ. Those of drooping habit will be planted near the pool's edge. Wisteria may be trained to droop its graceful fronds over and into the water.

Rhododendron and mountain laurel are indispensable both for their blossoms, which reflect into the water mirror, and for their foliage, which is rich and clean the year around. A good deal of leaf mold and acid soil should be worked in around these shrubs.

Ferns, in varying heights and form, are

among the most desirable of water-neighboring plants. Always decorative, rich in form, they are a graceful step between shrubbery and edging plants. Here again use plenty of leaf mold. Ferns may be purchased from nurseries which specialize in wild plants, or they may be gathered locally if available. They should be transplanted in the early spring before the delicate fronds have started to uncurl. At that time the plant is much like a clod of earth and may easily be handled.

There are many kinds of lilies that grow about three feet in height. Some of these desirable flowers will fit into complete sunlight or partial shade. They like cool feet and for this reason should be planted among ferns or low evergreens. Best known among these graceful plants are the regal, speciosium magnificum, and auratum.

Again in reference to smaller shrubs and plants may I suggest that you consider carefully local wild plants as well as those from nurseries. A complete scheme of wild plants may be most attractive and sensible. Explore the neighboring streams and woods for material, and supplement your gathered plants with nursery stock, especially for blooming sorts.

For the smaller edging plants I recommend

violets, creeping Jenny, ivy, lily-of-the-valley, dwarf iris, and small ferns. The nursery will provide ajuga, one of the best of all edging plants. Ajuga multiplies rapidly, one small plant spreading web-like feelers and producing a score of off-shoots in a season.

Ajuga is especially good at the water's edge in place of turf, which is hard to mow and soaks up much moisture, constantly lowering the water. In spring ajuga produces low spikes of beautiful blue flowers, and then the foliage develops into a thick mass of green bronze, lasting until frost.

The finest edging plant under overhanging shrubs where shade dominates is pachysandra, the most useful of all shade-loving ground covers. This plant seems immune from disease, is evergreen, and cares not at all for sunlight. Rooted cuttings develop in one year into good-sized plants; where masses are desired and economy is necessary, use these cuttings. Mature potted plants are more satisfactory where a few specimens are needed. Pachysandra propagates by sending out root feelers underground. These come through the surface and produce new plants.

Sedums are among the most desirable of plants for quick growth and as "softeners" over masonry and rockwork. There are hundreds of varieties, from the commonest sarmentosum to the choicer, finer forms. An amateur gardener friend of mine recently remarked that he liked sedum sarmentosum because it couldn't be discouraged. That is a necessary type of plant in every beginner's garden, and serves its purpose. Sedum sarmentosum certainly grows well anywhere; in fact it needs drastic thinning out the second season.

Iris, especially the dwarf varieties, are fine pool-edging plants. They establish themselves readily and give a good effect for minimum expense and care. In recommending iris, I think of the summer-long effect of the foliage as well as the beauty of the blossoms. Iris leaves have a natural water-side appearance. Their vertical fans give contrast in masses of drooping, compact planting. The commoner, garden varieties of iris are fairly tall and should be planted at the back of the pool. Better still, they may be planted in clumps a few feet away from the water's edge. The dwarf varieties are excellent close to the edge.

The primulas are fine plants for both amateur and experienced gardeners. They are easily obtainable in a great variety of kinds and colors. Many are common, while others are little aristocrats. Primulas have low-growing clumps of foliage and flower blossoms in early spring.

Of the medium-height border plants, I suggest Mertensia virginica, with very early stems of blue and blue-violet flowers; bleeding heart, a delightful old-fashioned plant with sprays of delicate pink blossoms; trilliums and lady slippers thrive in shaded, woodsy soil.

SUMMARY

Again I suggest acquaintance with your local plant grower, and reading of the excellent plant catalogues advertised in garden magazines. In their profusely illustrated booklets you will find detailed descriptions of tried and trusted plants.

Avoid crowding your plants. Smaller plants are generally most effective in groups of three or more. Contrast of light flowers against dark foliage is desirable. White, yellow, and lighter blooms add a note of freshness and contrast to the garden scheme.

Each gardener must learn through experience over a few seasons what will grow best in his own soil and exposure. The beginner sometimes purchases those plants which are most attractively illustrated in the catalogues. If you want the place to look established quickly, choose those which have proved their local hardiness, and which will grow willingly under your own conditions.

For more complete information on landscape planning and planting, see Doubleday Garden Handbook No. 4—HOW TO PLAN THE HOME LANDSCAPE, and No. 6—TREES AND SHRUBS FOR THE SMALL PLACE, obtainable where you bought this Handbook.

CHAPTER VII

The Landscaping of the Formal Pool

THE formal or semi-formal pool calls for an entirely different treatment than the natural or informal. True, it is possible for one pool to combine both types, but usually it is wiser to build your pool to be either one or the other, rather than a conglomerate.

The formal or semi-formal pool suggests a geometric arrangement of edging and planting (Figs. 21 and 22). Generally the edging material will be of slate or flat stone laid closely together or slightly at random, with grass between. These may be the width of a walk or as wide as a dining terrace, blending pool and neighboring building together. If the dwelling is brick, it is appropriate to have the same material surround the pool.

Frequently a pivotal point or center of interest is desired in connection with the formal pool.

FIG. 21. A FORMAL POOL WELL PLACED AND PLANTED

Straight lines, paved terraces, clipped hedges, and balanced plantings are appropriate for the rectangular pool placed near the house.

FIG. 22. A SEMI-FORMAL POOL NEAR THE HOUSE

Round or elliptical pools belong in the formal lawn or
garden and may be the terminal feature of a straight walk
from the porch or door. Slate edging is appropriate here.

This may be a vertical spray or water coming from an exposed fountain cowl. At one end of the pool a low wall fountain and spout may be built (Fig. 16, bottom). A simple piece of sculpture, a large piece of pottery, or a distinctive tree or shrub also serves. Inexpensive, appropriate cast garden sculpture is manufactured by several firms.

In general, neighboring borders, paths, and arbors should run parallel to the lines of the pool itself.

Planting may be in rigid, straight-lined borders, or more at random. A few smaller plants between the bordering stones are suggested to blend gracefully the water and surrounding lawn. Larger plants and shrubs may be used in boxes and tubs at the pool's corners; an arrangement which would be ridiculous for the naturalistic pool.

Plants of a rather set and orderly character are in keeping, such as clipped box, privet, cedars, yew, and arborvitæ. All these need good soil, the same as in the informal scheme.

For more complete information on handling soils and fertilizers to grow plants, see Doubleday Garden Handbook No. 1—GARDENING FOR THE SMALL PLACE, obtainable where you bought this Handbook.

CHAPTER VIII

Furnishing the Pool

FURNISHING the interior of the pool is a fascinating experience. After the water has been drawn off several times over a period of two weeks, you are ready for plants and fish. These are necessary as scavengers, mosquito killers, and oxygenators, and if thoughtfully selected will keep your pool clear and clean. Most people think only of the ornamental aspect of pool furnishing.

In a pool, all living things, including plants, are divided into those which live completely under the water, those which live on the surface, and those living both below and above the surface. Each has a separate work to do. Choose from a good catalogue or at a reliable dealer's the plants and animals best suited to your own requirements.

First let us consider water plants. Naturally waterlilies head the list. These lovely flowers are commonly placed into two classes—hardy and tropical (Fig. 25, top). Tropicals are either day or night blooming. The day-blooming varieties close in the evening, while the night-blooming lilies unfold and remain open until the following morning. On dark days, the night lilies frequently bloom well into the afternoon.

Hardy lilies, as the name implies, may be left in the pool or tub all winter. Tropicals must be stored in the cellar or warmer quarters during the cold months.

PLANTING WATERLILIES

All waterlilies demand plenty of sunshine and warm, still water. They may be planted one to a box two feet square by one foot deep (Fig. 23). The top of the box should be only six to eight inches below the surface of the water in order to benefit by the warming rays of the sun. If the pool is more than two feet deep, set boxes above the floor level on stones. It is best to have only one lily in a box of this size, and to have these boxes four or five feet apart as the average leaf spread is three feet.

Hardy lilies may be planted after all danger of freezing is past, while tropicals should not be placed outside until the water has become thoroughly warmed by the sun's rays. Tropicals do best in water of about eighty degrees.

Waterlilies are gross feeders and must be well fertilized. The best soil is a mixture of three parts fibrous loam or good garden soil with one

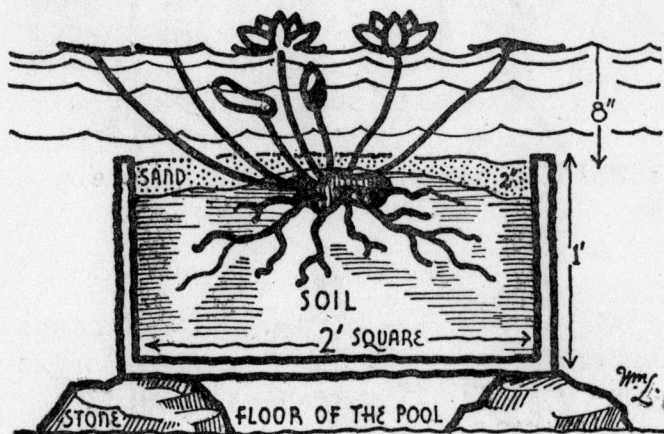

FIG. 23. HOW TO PLANT WATERLILIES

For each plant a box of good soil 2′ x 2′ x 1′ or its equivalent, four or five feet apart, blocked up to within eight inches of the water's surface in full sun. Sand on top keeps the water clear.

part of well-rotted cow manure. Never use fresh manure as it will ferment and stagnate the pool and injure plants. Or a prepared plant food may be mixed with the soil.

Place this prepared soil to within four inches of the top of the box. The lily root is then pressed just under the surface with the crown

POTAMOGETON

ANACHARIS

LUDWIGIA

WATER POPPY

CABOMBA

VALLISNERIA

FIG. 24. SOME DESIRABLE UNDERWATER PLANTS

These supply food, air, and shelter to fish and other denizens of the pool.

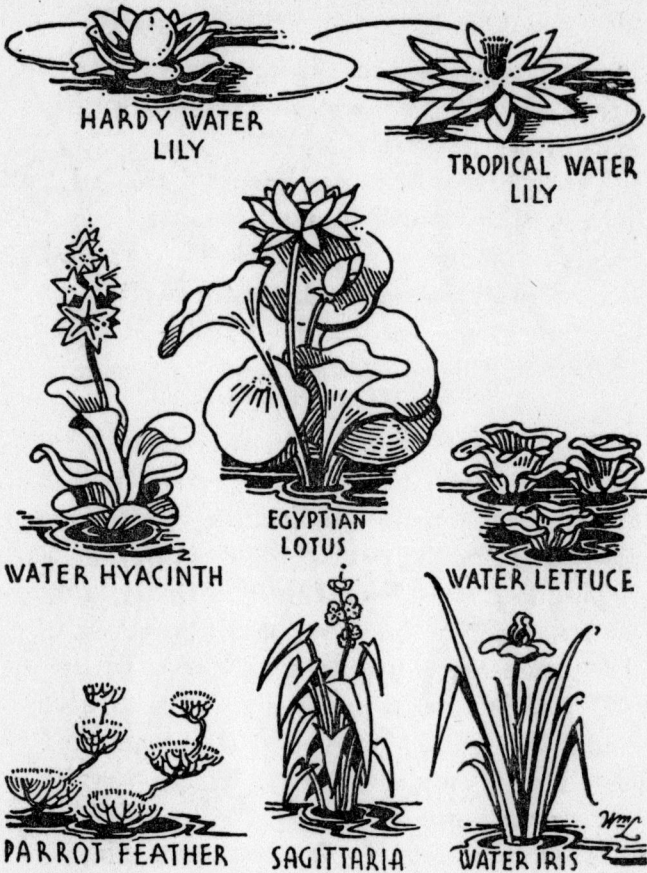

FIG. 25. PLANTS TO DECORATE THE POOL

Water hyacinth and water lettuce float on the surface, while the bog plants such as Egyptian lotus, parrot feather, pickerel rush, and water iris grow in shallow water or in the moist margins of the informal pool.

slightly exposed and an inch or two of sand sifted over all. The sand will keep the soil from discoloring the water.

When hardy lilies are left in a drained pool or tub, they should be well banked over with leaves or manure. If water is left in the pool, as is customary in ones which are well built, a cover of boards and leaves is ample.

UNDERWATER AND BOG PLANTS

Plants which grow under the water are usually oxygenators and supply oxygen and food to underwater life. Fish feed on their tender roots and leaves, and spawn in their tangled growth, hoping to protect their eggs from hungry frogs, turtles, and fish. Commonest and most useful in this group are cabomba, vallisneria, potamogeton, ludwigia, and anacharis. These are illustrated in Fig. 24. Many of these plants need no soil, it being only necessary to weight their lower ends to the bottom.

Another group of plants, among which are water poppy, water hyacinth, and water lettuce, float on the surface with fully exposed foliage and flowers (Fig. 25). The roots of these are fine for the fish. The floating plants soften the edge of the pool and blend border greens and water together.

Still another group of aquatic plants may be called the bog types, such as pickerel rush,

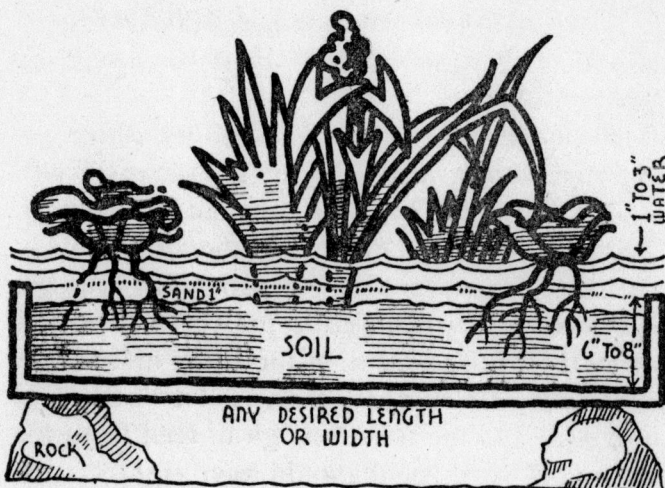

FIG. 26. HOW TO PLANT BOG PLANTS

Appropriate near the shallow edges of the pool, such plants as Egyptian lotus, parrot feather, pickerel rush, and water iris need six to eight inches of good soil with only an inch or two of water over them. A scattering of sand keeps the pool clear.

water iris, and Egyptian lotus (Fig. 25). These grow in soil covered by shallow water (Fig. 26), or in the very moist margins of the pool. They are highly desirable plants both for their grace of flower and foliage.

ANIMAL LIFE FOR THE POOL

Every pool in the fields and woods has its scavengers. These are both necessary and interesting in the garden pool. First in this group are fish.

Fish eat the hatching mosquitoes which inhabit any body of still water. Boards of Health and an interest in your own and neighbors' comfort demand these mosquito exterminators. Besides the common goldfish you can get Comets, Fantails, Telescopes, and Nymphs (Fig. 27), not to mention the many more kinds obtainable. They add life and color to the pool and soon become tame enough to feed from the fingers. A small pool should have eight or ten; a larger pool a greater number. Fish dealers can tell the sex of fish and if requested will supply the proper number of each for breeding.

There are several snails, large and small, of various colors including a rich red. Numbers of snails should be in every pool as they travel endlessly around the walls and stones, keeping the surface free of algæ and green scum.

Tadpoles are most useful, as they devour decayed matter and algæ.

Clams or fresh-water mussels need a few inches of soil to travel in. They feed on the

COMMON GOLD FISH

COMET TAIL

NYMPH

LION HEAD

TELESCOPE

CLAM

RED RAMSHORN SNAIL

AUSTRALIAN SNAIL

JAPANESE SNAIL

FROG

POLLIWOG

FIG. 27. INTERESTING AND USEFUL POOL DWELLERS

Various sorts of fish, snails, fresh-water clams, and frogs are easily obtainable for your pool.

solids and in doing so filter and clarify great quantities of water.

Frogs are said to eat fish eggs. Nevertheless, I feel that a frog or two lends much interest and personality to a pool. They also do a good job catching insects along its edges.

Turtles are interesting, but perhaps because of their weakness for tender, growing fish, they do not deserve a place in the garden pool.

CHAPTER IX

Hillside Pools and Brooks

FORTUNATE indeed is the gardener whose land lies in gradual or abrupt slopes. Here are possibilities for the pool or pools unique.

Most persons picture pools as in a perfectly flat location. Perhaps this conception comes from the waterlily catalogues where pools are generally pictured to show the best growing conditions for lilies. These same catalogues rather discourage the use of running water. They are right, as water plants in general prefer warm, still water.

If one can have either, it is difficult to choose between the still pool with waterlilies and the splashing, lively pool with its miniature waterfall. My own pool is entirely too shaded by beautiful dogwoods and oaks to grow lilies successfully, so I have the shade and the music of little streams of falling water as it drips or tumbles from pool to pool. Pickerel rush, water iris, parrot feather, water poppy, and many other plants thrive and bloom in these surroundings (Fig. 25). On a hot summer day or whenever I am working in the garden the music of running water is delightful.

PLACING

All the suggestions previously given as to location, planning, and construction apply equally in building hillside pools. A little less choice is usually possible in locating them, as the slope of the ground commonly determines the position.

The waterfalls should drop so as to be seen from the most important viewpoint, toward the porch, garden, or path of approach. This suggests the source pool high up in a background of shrubs, with an uninterrupted flow from somewhere beyond. A ledge of rocks or a twisted old stump makes a good source point (Fig. 29). Picture a spring issuing from a woodland hillside. That's exactly the effect to attain.

CONSTRUCTION

You might begin by scooping out roughly three or more basins of different size and at different levels (Fig. 28). Variety in size—smaller leading to the final larger pool at the base—is both attractive and logical from Nature's point of view. Different heights with drops of six inches to several feet mean just that number of tunes in so many keys. The little drips are high and tinkling. The longer drops have a rich mellow sound. The combination makes for a complete marine orchestra!

Excavate and build each pool as suggested in Chapter IV. Scoop deeply enough to allow for cinders and six inches of concrete. No forms are required but it is wise to use plenty of reinforcement. Heavy chicken wire is best, as it may be had wide enough to go into the small excavation in one piece. It can be held off the cinders by laying it on small stones. If it has a tendency to buckle up, drive a stake with a nail in it into the ground through the wire mesh until the nail catches and holds the wire down. This can be removed as the concrete is poured and as its weight holds the wire in place.

All concrete used in this kind of a pool should be colored to the tone of natural stone by using powdered lampblack. This may be secured from a builder's supply house, hardware store, or mason. Simply mix in the quantity desired for a darker shade. Remember that all concrete grows lighter in color as it dries. This same darker concrete can be used to model the lips on the overhanging rocks. Small pieces of flat stone

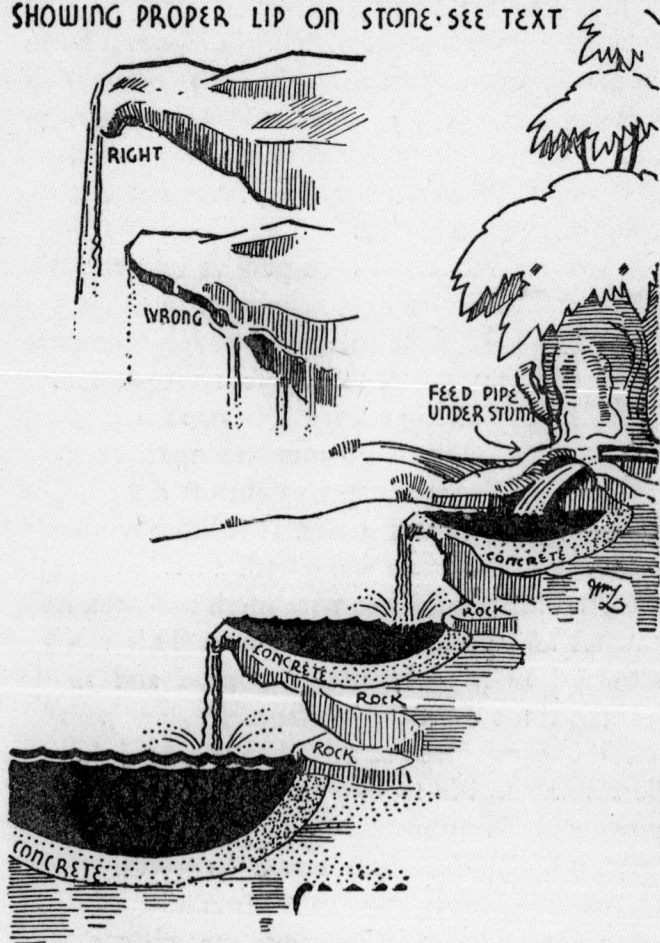

SHOWING PROPER LIP ON STONE · SEE TEXT

RIGHT

WRONG

FEED PIPE
UNDER STUMP

CONCRETE

ROCK

CONCRETE

ROCK

ROCK

CONCRETE

FIG. 28. CROSS SECTION OF HILLSIDE POOLS

Basins of different sizes and at different levels are easily
made, for a garden symphony of tinkling waterfalls.

FIG. 29. A SERIES OF SMALL POOLS ON A LITTLE HILLSIDE

Like a cool spring issuing from a woodland hillside such
a beauty spot is possible for any garden on a slope.

or thin copper bent into shape can be set in place and covered with cement. A few pebbles or rough sand dusted on the wet cement also assists the illusion of age and naturalness.

As a pool of this kind is not "standard," a considerable amount of studying and "fussing about" with rocks and grading is well spent before pouring concrete.

Fig. 28 shows an overhang for each pool so the water may fall clear to the pool below. This lip of the waterfall is most important. It must have a slight upgrade under the overhang to prevent the water flowing down the under side of the rock into the earth instead of dropping into the pool below. This overhang has another distinct advantage. It casts a dark shadow which makes for mystery and shows the slow stream of water to better advantage.

All rockwork built up under the pools should be firmly laid with some cement and into tamped, firm ground to preclude heaving and settling. As you progress in this grading of rocks and soil wet them down thoroughly to settle the earth.

The rocks surrounding the pools may be arranged as suggested in Chapter VI (and see Fig. 29). Since they may serve as partial foundations for the pool basins, special care

must be taken to establish them firmly. Follow
the ledge principle and tilt the rock back to
prevent washing by surface water. This also
directs the water to plant roots and keeps it
from running into the pool below to muddy
the water.

It is well to build at least the larger pool deep
enough for two or more goldfish, to take care of
the mosquitoes. A frequent flushing or the flow
of the water will wash the larvæ to the large
pool where fish will devour them. Better these
little pools with a distinct drop between them
than a meandering brook in which puddles collect along with the bugs.

WATER SUPPLY

This type of pool depends for its charm on a
permanent water supply, which can be provided
as suggested in Chapter III. It may be desirable
to use a larger copper tube than the quarter-
inch one recommended there.

If water is scarce or expensive a little return
pump may be installed. This makes it possible
to use the water over and over again. This
pump, an electrically driven, inexpensive machine, may be located in a "kennel" behind the
shrubbery, in a box underground, or in the
house cellar. We suggest consultation with

your near-by plumber or professional mechanic familiar with this type of equipment.

BOG GARDEN

A water supply suggests an outlet and an outlet suggests a bog garden (Fig. 11). In place of a drain-well, have the overflow run over one edge or through a length of pipe to the surrounding ground. This pipe can be set into the pool just below its rim to run singly or fan shape for several feet over the surrounding soil. Each pipe should be drilled with many holes to allow a ready and distributed disposal of water. Take the pipes to a garage or machine shop where there is a power drill and do the job in a few minutes.

The soil all around these pipes should be of "woods" quality, absorbent and marshy. A good deal of peat moss, dried leaves, or woods topsoil should be worked into the ground to a depth of eighteen inches. You now have an ideal place for water iris, cowslips, cardinal flower, cattails, and dozens of other attractive plants. You only have to examine the margins of the nearest pond to assure yourself that the bog or marsh garden is a study by itself.

A few frogs will make life miserable for the

flying things which like this damp ground. The frogs also add personality to the garden. Give them names and get acquainted with Old Tom, Mossy, Leaping Lena, and the rest of the frog family.

CHAPTER X

Care of the Pool

ONCE established, the pool demands very little care. Aphis do collect on the waterlilies. These may be flushed off with the hose and make excellent fish food. The stray dog or cat may take too active an interest and must be "shooed" off with broom and water.

Where there are very young children, precautions should be taken against accident. The pool should be separated from the play yard by a light wire fence or a coarse mesh wire may be fastened from wall to wall of the pool just under the water's surface.

If the water becomes murky after hard rains, it usually clears in a day or two, or may be changed quickly by a hose flushing.

A net on a bamboo pole will come in handy in removing foreign matter.

The leaves which fall into the water will sink eventually and serve as a blanket for frogs and snails. In the spring the water may be drained off and all this débris sorted and carted away.

During the freezing months it is wise to cover the pool with boards and a generous layer of leaves. This is all the protection needed for the plant and animal life.

Our parting wish is that you have built your pool carefully and that no cracks appear after the first winter. Cracks cannot be permanently mended; but they may be scraped out and re-filled with wet concrete as a temporary repair.

INDEX